Snowy Egrets Skim the Lake
Poetry & Prose

Jeanette McClelland

Selected & Edited by
Ted Wojtasik

Copyright © The Estate of Jeanette McClelland 2015

All Rights Reserved

No part of this work may be reproduced or transmitted in any form or by any means, electronic or mechanical, including photocopying and recording, or by any information storage or retrieval system without the proper written permission of the copyright owner unless such copying is expressly permitted by federal copyright law.

Cover Art: Rooney Coffman
Typesetter & Designer: Ted Wojtasik
Proofreader: Madge McKeithen

All photographs courtesy of the
Estate of Jeannette McClelland
and Tom Patterson

ISBN-13: 978-1517026301
ISBN-10: 151702630X

sa UNIVERSITY PRESS

St. Andrews University Press

St. Andrews University Press
(A branch of Webber International University)
St. Andrews University
1700 Dogwood Mile
Laurinburg, NC 28352
press@sa.edu
(910) 277-5310

Editorial Board

Paul Baldasare
Joseph Bathanti
Richard Blanco
Betsy Dendy
Robert Hopkins
Edna Ann Loftus
Madge McKeithen
Ted Wojtasik

Ted Wojtasik, Editor
Madge McKeithen, Assistant Editor

Ronald H. Bayes, Founding Editor
1969

Dedicated to

Everyone who loved, supported, and believed in
Jeanette McClelland
(1953-1977)

16th Birthday   High school senior photo   Jeanette with her new car
1968   1971   1977
All in Springfield, VA

Table of Contents

Introduction

After a Picture of Jeanette McClelland 1
Tom Patterson

Dedication

to remember Jeanette McClelland 7
Mark Smith

Poetry

Before Dawn 9
Quail 10
Frightened 11
Hawk Stoops 12
In the Field 13
Not 14
Kensington Gardens 15
After a Dream of Smithfield 16
We Meet 17
The Accident 18
So Much Ketchup 19
That Day in Winter 20
For Adrianne Marcus 21

The Posthumous Travels of Evita Peron 22

Remember 23

When Haz 24

Sun Glints Warm on Ice 25

Winter Sun Shining 26

Jealousy 27

In Time 28

October 1974: Mt. Mitchell 29

Sour Grass and Love to Mary Jane 30

Flight 31

Fiction

Miss Williams and the Dinosaur 32

Envoi

The Last 40

Biographical Sketch 41

Notes 43

Jeanette McClelland "in comic mode"

After a Picture of Jeanette McClelland

Tom Patterson

In every house or apartment I've lived in since the late 1970s I've found a prominent spot for a special photograph of my late friend and fellow writer Jeanette McClelland. This informal portrait captures her in comic mode, kneeling on a grassy lawn and grinning mischievously, her arms outstretched and fingers curled like the claws of a B-movie monster poised to attack. Our friend Melissa Tufts made the photo and gave me this high-contrast print of it as a gift while Jeanette was still with us. I've customarily hung it high on a wall where it's easily seen—not only as a reminder of a close, fun-loving friend gone far too soon from this life, but also as a source of personal inspiration. I like to imagine her watching over me from that elevated perspective, observing the course of my life and writing career like a guardian spirit or muse.

Jeanette and I were both English majors and creative-writing students at St. Andrews when we met, and our writing aspirations played a big part in our friendship. I was a year older and one academic year ahead of her, so we weren't in the same classes, but we studied under most of the same teachers, and lived in the same dormitory during my senior year.

Unaffected and unpretentious, Jeanette didn't go out of her way to call attention to herself, but she excelled academically and distinguished herself as one of the school's most promising poets. As our friendship developed, I came to appreciate the close attention she paid to the world around her, and her sensitivity to the feelings, personalities and ideas of her friends and associates. Inherently curious and possessed of an adventurous spirit, she also struck me as more emotionally grounded than many of our young contemporaries—wise beyond her years.

As editor of *Cairn*, the student literary magazine, I published three of Jeanette's poems in the 1973-74 issue. According to St. Andrews tradition at that time, the magazine's editor was always a senior student who served for one year and handpicked the next year's editor. When it was my turn to pick a successor, Jeanette was the obvious choice, and she turned in an impressive performance with the 1974-75 issue. (Full disclosure: The issue contains some of my own writings and drawings, including the cover drawing of a bull crossbred with a tuba.)

Jeanette and I corresponded and saw each other occasionally after I graduated in 1974 and she followed suit in 1975. Our last visit was under memorable circumstances in January 1976. Accompanied by another friend from the South, I was driving back from New York, where we'd attended a benefit reading for the *St. Andrews Review* at the legendary Gotham Book Mart. Jeanette was living with her parents at their house in the Virginia suburbs of Washington, D.C., and on very short notice they were kind enough to let us spend a night at their house on our way through. That evening Jeanette took us out to a party hosted by a co-worker at the press where she was employed. Back at her house later, we stayed up into the wee hours talking.

I was out of the country for five of the sixteen months that remained of Jeanette's life. We exchanged a few letters and postcards during that interval, and then suddenly she was gone under the most brutal of circumstances, so alien to everything else about her life up to those unimaginable final moments.

I certainly remember where I was when I found out—visiting my own parents in Georgia. It was Melissa Tufts who reached me there by phone to deliver the heartbreaking news. A few days later we all gathered—as many of her close friends as could arrange to be there—with her former teachers at St. Andrews to read aloud from Jeanette's poems and tributes we had written in her memory. Several of the poems in this volume were read on that occasion, at which Mark Smith also read his new poem fittingly republished as this book's dedication.

To have Jeanette's poems and the short story gathered under this one cover is a priceless gift to those of us who knew and loved her—and to readers who never had that privilege. Reading the digital proof of the book for the first time—and several times since then—has been a powerful *deja vu* experience. I remembered almost everything here on first (re)reading, despite the passage of almost 40 years since I last looked at most of them. A number of the poems, especially the first several, reflect the strong influence of the traditional Japanese poetic forms our mentor Ron Bayes emphasized in his creative-writing classes. I wouldn't be surprised if some of them weren't written as assignments for those classes.

The emphasis on nature imagery in Jeanette's poems is also characteristic of the Japanese tradition. Most of her nature-grounded poems reflect her experience of the landscape at and around St. Andrews. With its tranquil lake and cypress swamp, the school was in the early 1970s still largely surrounded by rural farmland, the cotton fields and pine plantations of the Carolina Sandhills.

I am uniquely qualified to at least partially explicate Jeanette's most enigmatic and amusing poem, "After a Dream of Smithfield." The title of course tells us we're not in the ordinary waking world here, and she almost surely had the referenced dream at St. Andrews, which is about 90 miles from the town of Smithfield, North Carolina. But the poem also appropriates and riffs on several lines from some nonsense writings I composed on Jeanette's typewriter during a small gathering of friends in her dorm room one evening at St. Andrews. On separate index cards I found alongside the typewriter, I began writing very brief, spontaneous, stream-of-consciousness portraits or descriptions of each person in the room, including Jeanette, Ned Leager, Charlie Hart and my younger brother Hunter Patterson, along with a few others. In each piece I left out most of the vowels in the subject's name and throughout the series I adopted a chopped variation on southern dialect. The whole project occupied me for no more than 20 minutes while everyone else was talking and drinking and laughing. My 'DESCRIP O' JNT MCLND,' as I titled it, took off from an old snapshot in Jeanette's room, which showed her as a tiny child standing in what looked like a bucket. Hence, "She standin in dat dam bucket or Whatebba you callem," as I wrote. And "He wuik at dat hahtware sto," is from my "descrip o'" Ned Leager, which also contains a phrase Jeanette uses to conclude the poem, "the sons a Luke."

One line compacts the title of "Oh Dem Watermelons," Robert Nelson's legendary independent film from 1965, spoofing racist stereotypes of African Americans. With its earworm soundtrack—an extended faux minstrel tune by avant-garde composer Steve Reich, of all people—the film had recently been screened at St. Andrews, maybe even earlier on the evening of that session in Jeanette's room. It would certainly help to explain the wacky mood we were all in. (Of course you can now watch the film online: https://www.youtube.com/watch?v=lvs0-nPNha8).

So, yes, indeed, this volume brings back a torrent of personal memories, only a few of which I've mentioned here—in addition to the overriding memory of what a promising writer Jeanette McClelland was. I hope her example serves to inspire other young writers fortunate enough to find this little book in their hands.

—Winston-Salem, North Carolina
November 2015

to remember Jeanette McClelland

May 1977

Mark Smith

A smile of bone skin
often washed
across her dogwood eyes flagrantly, her cheeks,
her welcome, broad motion
welcomed forever, it felt.

Make remembered!

Rinse the rich hair
that lit up her forehead,
toweled her wry mellowness,
that whet our cafeteria grace!

Today damp beauty, South as
heat and light,
orange and green,
unshoulders me under
twenty some stone.

Thirty cypress, Jeanette,
where you lived
soak, without life,
into the drenched,
anachronistic air

our loss;

our own vital fluid
we lace with care, such
for our sakes
gasp in helpless, sweaty
rage, damned damn impropriety!

Your dignity denied, we
invoke humanity, your honor,
the kiss you implanted where we
(unable to)
will not displace it!

Before Dawn

Before dawn
snowy egrets skim the lake
echoing the moon curve
into cool cypress.

Quail

Quail—
Seven at least
In startled staccato
Like the cold crack of a wet sheet
Take wing.

Frightened

Frightened
oystercatcher
with feathers bold black/white
shivers silently beneath my
cold hands.

Hawk Stoops

hawk stoops
with a startle
down carmine curved mountain;
wings spread will eclipse the valley
below.

In the Field

In the field
There is the house embraced
By pink flowered cotton
That insists itself gently
Before the defoliation.

Sagging roof
Curves toward the time
When the field
Will make its final
Statement.

Not

This place, this face
I outline with fingers strong with Not—
Not know, not have, not not want.
You will not sense the heart cut.
We are walking all the time
Through white birch and treeless heath;
I cannot see the Tower.

Half hidden in four hours sleeping, this place,
Where I touch hands of no substance,
Of more shadow than a dream of England
In North Carolina.
We are walking all the time
Down one way winter streets
As narrow as that time we had.

I wish to see you golden green, but now
You are as though you could be
But never will, for Not is not
A passing strength, is weaker I.
We are walking all the time
Speaking words convincing
As a damn Georgian bridge.

Princess, ice-bound in mocking jade,
I would enter streets not yours
Unless you choose, with proper provision.
The direction of the traffic is not known.
We are walking all the time
In this distant country that no longer exists,
And I cannot see the Tower.

Kensington Gardens

Across the bridge to Charing Cross
The harmonica man plays to the jingle
Of coins that I wanted for buying
Flowers (for you or me, just so
We'd have 'em).
The train then, to Notting Hill Gate
(the highest heath
still keeps the tower in sight)
And wander in silence through fields
Where afghans sport in seersucker trousers
And kangaroos race the palace green.

After a Dream of Smithfield

Down streets before ourselves, you lead
To the train station lined with carcasses where
She standin in dat dam bucket or
Whatebba you callem, slipping on
Wet, pink, ohdemwatermelon guts.
He wuik at dat hahtware sto.,
"Martin & Sons, Offal Salesman."
Hard wear on the feet, I tell you,
It's a mess, ain't it?
Hanging out at St. Bart's,
The dog name of Quohog Hobo
Stops a minute where Rahere
Ate a bit of cheese and saw
Marley's ghost.
Now that Frenchie lie under a cairn of coal,
Nothing to show for that dream
But a wooden box for your ten pence, please.
And it's a little bit chilly but
You got enough turtles around your neck
To warm all the sons a Luke.

We Meet

we meet,
move away,
making patterns
that shape our lives, not
thinking.

return,
leave again,
never knowing
when will come the next
meeting.

The Accident

A car, hurtling into a cliff,
Screams once.
And death comes down.
Curious people stare
But turn away, chest thudding
As broken children die.
A red lantern glows fitfully,
Shaming the place with its lurid glare.
And a lonely policeman
Sweeps up the glass.

So Much Ketchup

At the death of a friend
We stand, remember,
And give thanks for life.
One death, or two, can touch us, but
Not bold type headlines multiplying pain
Endlessly.
Fourteen Arabs murdered,
Eleven Israelis,
What matter; the numbers are faceless.

Sipping beer in the den
We watch as TV pans
The violated room, where death snuck in
Like a jackal.
Scuffed brown shoes lonely
By the bed, blood spattered
On the walls; too much blood, like
So much ketchup.
Yawning, reach for a French fry.

That Day in Winter

That day in winter
when cold clutched
the death-blooming trees,
and brittle-veined leaves
shattered harshly in the wind,
I stood at my window
and traced ice initials on the glass,
then covered them with my hand
so you would not be cold.

For Adrianne Marcus

Sister, your
ruthless honesty holds
a moment of your life
and looks, unflinching—
puts it down
and picks up
another.

You invite me to look
through your eyes, then
leave me there and look
yourself, through another's.
Moses, Columbus,
your words, their eyes.

Sister, your
truth burns cold light
through dark words.
My heart follows
your syllables
and you become
what you say.

The Posthumous Travels of Evita Peron

When the military
ousted Peron
in 1955, Evita's
corpse
(magnificently embalmed
for a $100,000 fee by
a Spanish pathologist)
was shuttled by govt. agents
from one
secret hiding place to
another.
Only in 1971 was the
body
(still in excellent
condition despite
a smashed nose,
two (2) broken knees
and a haircut)
returned to Peron
for burial on the grounds
of his Spanish
villa.

Remember

remember
that summer after—
was it, seventh grade?
mud-sliding down suicide trail
in our white shorts.
never did get 'em clean, did we?
and oh! the secret notes from Sham.
we thought that was a cool name
til we found out the sham was
really those sticky notes we
gentled under our pillows at night
written by the girl in the next tent.
we used her training bras for
kite tails. we were neat.
then you left, friend,
sucked into eighth grade
a long ways from mine.
we knew nothing would change.
we wrote for three years,
then met again for a weekend.
it was a long weekend.

When Haz

when haz
eltrees bow
   (late in
the wind)
then rosily
sunset
bespeaks sudden
       rain.

Sun Glints Warm on Ice

sun glints warm on ice.
     melting snow bares dark, fresh earth.
 a winter over.

Winter Sun Shining

Winter sun shining
Like warm, friendly destruction
Melts lone snow patches.

Jealousy

I was eating cherry Jello at the time
   And still saw green.
    Green.

In Time

In time of clear, sharp-
taloned Fear, comes the choosing
of sides and honor.

October 1974: Mt. Mitchell

We four
have come a distance
to watch late sun
lie russet over
October hills.

Low rain clouds have
met us here
and blotted out warmth
and that color.
With now narrow focus on
clammy fingered pines dripping moss
in twisted supplication,
we put our heads back
and the rain slants scented silver
down our throats.

We stand as the drops
tremble on our lashes,
then concede to gravity
and splash our cheeks.

Sour Grass and Love to Mary Jane

In that summer,
When clouds ran and
Formed together separately
I lay (like the Fool on the Hill)
And watched
Lions become mermaids and
Huge sea monsters turn into
Mary Jane-next-door.

Like sun-bleached earth I lay,
And gloried in the living.
Plucked sour grass from the hill
And pretended I was old enough
To smoke.
Blowing make-believe smoke rings,
I watched them become
Mary Jane-next-door.

In that summer,
When hills were for rolling down,
And the purpose of knees was to be scraped,
I laughed and loved,
And gave sour grass and dandelions
To Mary Jane-next-door.

Flight

When contest wages
And distant hills speak thunder,
Then shall I
      (in muchness of tears bitter-
hard)
Travel windward on the level plain.

Like leafy young moss
I lie on the bank—
      Fresh thoughts
      greening in the sun.

Miss Williams and the Dinosaur

Miss Williams and Mlle. Nasta had met as pen pals. They were now each fifty-three years old but Miss Williams was the elder by four months and by virtue of the fact that of the two she had come closer to being married. She had been jilted when she was thirty six, an experience which had invested her with a sonorous dignity. She was a large woman with tremendous breasts that she carried like they were two tanks on a box car. The size of her bust provided Miss Williams with a secret revenge. Melvin E. Baker Jr., to whom she had been engaged for seven years, lived only three miles away from her with a wife who was undeniably flat. At every social occasion where she might possibly run into Melvin E. Baker Jr. Miss Williams wore a large corsage mounted sturdily over her left bosom. She liked the added dimension. Though she spoke often of the injustice that had been done her, and even measured time by the years she would have been married, the revenge she took with her bra size was now a perfunctory ritual, and she secretly liked the way things had turned out.

For one thing, during the three months when she was not teaching seventh-grade English at Washington Irving Junior High School she was completely free to do whatever she wanted. She took some pains to mask the freedom she enjoyed; out of habit she felt it her civic duty and moral obligation to hound Melvin E. Baker Jr. whenever possible. In addition to the orchid-on-the-bosom device, there was one torment that Miss Williams particularly relished. Melvin E. Baker Jr. was the president of the PTA, whose monthly meetings gave her ample opportunity for ingenious harassment. She had recently hit upon a new one, and she was ready with it tonight. It had become the custom at the last meeting of the school year for the teachers to tell each other where they were going for the summer. Most said that they were going to the beach for a week or to visit their parents in Omaha. Miss Williams always did something exciting, though in keeping with her image she managed to make it appear that she had no choice in the matter. Tonight she fixed a haughty eye on Melvin E. Baker Jr. and announced that she was not sure if she were going to the Barbados or Alaska. (She noticed with satisfaction that Melvin E. Baker Jr. grimaced at this—she knew he would spend his summer paying for braces.) She continued, with a slight adjustment to her corsage, to say that her French pen pal was definitely coming tomorrow to spend several weeks "to improve her English; the poor thing probably makes hideous conversation."

When Miss Williams drove home from the PTA meeting her thoughts were still on the upcoming visit of Mlle. Nasta. She would pick her up at National Airport the next afternoon at 1:32, Pan Am Flight 973. She was certainly glad she was a Washingtonian, it gave one a definite advantage she thought. Especially when dealing with Europeans. She figured that Washington cancelled out Lyon, even if it was in France. She couldn't imagine living anywhere else. She had a firm idea that no one in the rest of the country knew anything that was going on. She often unwittingly infuriated her friends by writing to them three days after a national event and asking if they had heard about it. She felt fully prepared to show her city to Mlle. Nasta, but she did hope that the French-woman had sensible shoes. She had an idea that Mlle.

Nasta was an aging Parisian model with gray hair and tight shoes.

Miss Williams arrived at the airport twenty minutes early the next afternoon. It was very hot. She tugged at her dress and sat down in the Pan Am lounge. Her stockings were bagging around the ankles. She tried to fix them discreetly, but saw that it was going to be a major operation. She pulled herself to her feet and headed for the ladies room. When she returned the loudspeaker was announcing Mlle. Nasta's flight. Miss Williams hoped that she would recognize her guest, for they had never exchanged pictures. At fifty three, neither of them were particularly interested in current photographs.

Miss Williams recognized Mlle. Nasta only because she heard her speaking English to the stewardess. She stood back a moment and looked at her guest; first impressions were most important. Mlle. Nasta was anything but a Parisian model, aging or not. She was an unstarched counterpart to Miss Williams, her body sagging in every structural part. She wore a limp black dress that contrasted with Miss Williams's bold red and blue checked suit. Her hair poked crazily out of her small gray hat, which itself was flattened from the force of nine hours in the corner of an airplane seat. Her shoes were satisfactory, if plain. Miss Williams noted the remaining details of her costume and then focused on the large book Mlle. Nasta clutched in her arms. She judged this to be a dictionary from the way the woman was flipping hastily through it. She realized that her guest needed assistance and stepped forward to take command of the situation.

"*Bonjour*," said Miss Williams firmly to Mlle. Nasta. She pronounced this to rhyme with "sewer." Their letters to each other had never leaned heavily toward literary scholarship, and Miss Williams's conversational abilities were no better. The only reason Miss Williams could communicate in French was that she refused to believe that anyone could not understand her. She simply lunged into a conversation, sprinkling it liberally with expressions like "*d'accord?*" and "*zut, alors!*" She liked to think she had a grasp of the vernacular. Now, with this belief welcome, Miss Williams dismissed the French language. Sink or swim, she thought to herself; Mlle. Nasta had come to learn English.

"Glad t'meet you," Miss Williams continued, "I'm Marion Williams.

"Thank you very much," said Mlle. Nasta with obvious relief. "You are very kind. I am very glad to meet you." This seemed to be the only English she had on tap at the moment, and she lapsed into silence.

Miss Williams picked up the conversation. "Bags," she said. "We'll get your bags. Down this way." Mlle. Nasta followed obediently.

Miss Williams retrieved the luggage without incident; however, others on the flight were not so fortunate. As the suitcases came out of the loading area, they fell heavily onto a circular conveyor belt. One large black Samsonite bag burst open to reveal red hearts that patterned a pair of men's boxer shorts. The waiting passengers seized upon this diversion. Those in the back craned their necks as the suitcase went around and around, exposing more of its contents with each revolution. Everyone waited to see who would claim it.

As an airline official came out to retrieve the suitcase, there was a general murmur of disappointment.

Miss Williams did not join in the conversation of the underwear. She was busy thinking. She had not counted on having to labor for topics of conversation with Mlle. Nasta. True, the woman had barely arrived, but Miss Williams was always uncomfortable at the possibility of not having anything to say. She pondered this problem as she hefted two of Mlle. Nasta's three suitcases and made her way to the car. She was weaving between the taxi cabs in front of the North Terminal, with Mlle. Nasta trudging along behind, when the idea struck her.

"Art!" she exclaimed. Mlle. Nasta glanced up, startled, but Miss Williams did not notice. Art would certainly be a common interest and besides, it would get Mlle. Nasta's visit off on the right cultural foot. She would take her for a visit to the National Gallery before they went home. She had led many seventh graders there on field trips—children who snickered loudly in the silence of the museum and nervously averted their eyes when confronted by imposing collections of ancient nudity. She was pleased that she did not have the responsibility for them today. Miss Williams located the car and stowed the luggage and Mlle. Nasta inside.

Miss Williams found that it was even more difficult to find a parking place at the National Gallery than it had been to find one at the airport. She finally edged her blue Pinto station wagon into a space on the far side of the Mall that had been previously occupied by a Volkswagen. She turned to Mlle. Nasta and noted with satisfaction that she was already showing more enthusiasm than she had demonstrated at the airport.

"We have a little way to walk, I'm afraid," said Miss Williams somewhat loudly. She had a vague idea, which she never would have admitted to, that the inability to understand the English language must be related to a defect of the ear.

"That is very nice. You are very kind," said Mlle. Nasta cheerfully. She held on to her dictionary tightly as they set off down the street.

They walked for nearly five minutes, threading their way through several groups of Japanese tourists and busloads of children from Fredericksburg and Baltimore. Miss Williams was hotter than she had been at the airport. Her stockings were wrinkling around her ankles again. They walked in silence until they were within a block of the National Gallery. Then Mlle. Nasta pointed interestedly at a large statue of a dinosaur which some children were climbing on and asked what the name of it was in English. Miss Williams took the dictionary from her as they continued to walk and began to look up the word. She could have simply told her the name, but she realized that she might as well accustom herself to that particular dictionary because it appeared that Mlle. Nasta would be referring to it often. She was beginning to wonder if Mlle. Nasta had employed a ghost writer in the years of their correspondence.

Miss Williams propped the dictionary on the wide shelf of her chest and peered nearsightedly at the small print. The word did not appear to be there. This made her slightly uneasy; she wanted to be able to depend on that dictionary. She looked again—"din, dine, ding-dong ..." As Miss Williams concentrated on the page, she reached the end of the block, tripped over the curb and fell heavily into the street. Mlle. Nasta gasped. Miss Williams yelled. Everyone on the street turned and stared. Miss Williams got to her feet as soon as possible, assisted by Mlle. Nasta, who was talking excitedly in French. She hobbled to a nearby park bench and sat down to inventory the damage. There was a large hole in the knee of her stocking, and a scrape of the same size on the knee itself. The ankle of that leg was beginning to throb badly. Mlle. Nasta then handed her the heel of her shoe.

"Good grief," said Miss Williams in disgust. Mlle. Nasta had run out of French exclamations, and stood quietly holding the heel. It would have been a relief to yell some more, but Miss Williams thought she had called enough attention to herself. She looked through her purse for a Kleenex to mop up the blood which was oozing down her leg. She settled for one that had been used on a previous occasion. As she rested on the park bench, she thought about what to do. The gallery was closer now than the car and it would be cool there; she decided they would continue. She stood up, put the heel in her purse, and arranged her skirt to cover her knee as best she could. She limped across the street, followed by Mlle. Nasta and the dictionary.

By the time Miss Williams climbed the steps and shuffled through the revolving door of the gallery, she regretted her decision to continue the excursion. She was perspiring and her leg hurt. She looked around for a place to sit down. She noticed several wheel chairs leaning against the far wall of the room. She looked at them thoughtfully and weighed the pros and cons to her dignity. She decided that the image of a vigorous invalid was preferable to that of a disheveled ambulant. She limped purposefully across the room and unfolded the nearest wheelchair. Settling herself into the chair, she noticed Mlle. Nasta's dictionary and said crossly, "Dinosaur. It was a dinosaur." She assumed a look of impassive arrogance and motioned for Mlle. Nasta to follow her.

The Last

the last
time i saw you
you left me a smile
that will warm my winters until
i die

Biographical Sketch

Jeanette McClelland was born on December 10, 1953, in Washington, DC, and grew up in Northern Virginia. She graduated from West Springfield High School in 1971. Mrs. Barbara Ostrowski, her high school English teacher, influenced Jeanette to pursue English and creative writing as a college major and as a career. She had several poems published in her high school literary magazine, *The Symposium*.

Jeanette attended St. Andrews Presbyterian College (now St. Andrews University) and graduated with a B.A. degree in English in 1975. That same year she was also the winner of the Alan Bunn Memorial Chapbook Competition for her collection of poems titled *In the Middle Way*. In addition she was the student editor of the student literary journal *Cairn* from 1974-1975.

Following college graduation, Jeanette completed a graduate course in Editing from George Washington University, and she worked as a proofreader at Bryd Press. To all who remember her, Jeanette had a beautiful smile, an adventurous spirit, and a generous heart. She volunteered in Laurinburg, NC, helping children with homework assignments. She used the occasion of Christmas and birthdays to gift new clothes to children of low-income families. She is remembered for regularly reading bedtime stories and singing bedtime lullabies to her much younger sister, Sarah. Jeanette's life ended abruptly and tragically in May 1977. She has been sorely missed, ever since, by her parents, her four younger sisters, and her innumerable friends.

Jeanette McClelland, in black fedora and plaid shirt,
gives a thumbs up with her friend.
Laurinbug, NC, 1975

Jeanette with her father
Alexandria, VA, winter, 1953-1954

Notes

"Flight," "The Accident," and the three haiku—"Winter Sun Shining," "Jealousy," "In Time,"—appeared in *The Symposium*, the literary journal of West Springfield High School (1970). The poem "Sour Grass and Love to Mary Jane" appeared in the *Cairn*, vol. 8 (1972), the poem "The Last" appeared in the *Cairn*, vol. 10 (1973-1974), and the short story "Miss Williams and the Dinosaur" appeared in the *Cairn*, vol. 12 (1976). All the other poems appeared in her chapbook *In the Middle Way* (1975), some in different versions first published in the *Cairn*.

	Born	Passed
Dad born	1912	2004
Uncle Bob born	1926	2022
Marcy	1940	
Kathy McNellis	1954	

```
 1940 - Marcy born
-  14
─────────
 1926 - Uncle Bob born
+  96
─────────
 2022 - Uncle Bob passed


  1926 - Uncle Bob born
-   14
─────────
  1912 - Dad born - 6/9/1912
```